Audaciously YOU!

52 Boldness Boosting Strategies to Help Unleash the Warrior in You!

Tonoa Bond

AIM High Media & Publishing

Tonoa Bond

AIM High Media & Publishing

Audaciously YOU!: 52 Boldness Boosting Strategies to Help Unleash the Warrior in You!

By: Tonoa Bond, MS

Published in the United States of America by:
AIM High Media & Publishing (Subsidiary of McLaughlin-Bond International)
6140 Highway 6 South; #259
Missouri City, TX 77459
www.AimHighPub.com

ISBN: 978-1-942962-07-6
Library of Congress Control: 2016933939

This title is also available on:
Kindle & iBooks, and as an AIM High Publishing eBook.

Cover Photo: Jamicia Ware
Cover Design: Ihor Tureha
Interior Design: AIM High Media & Publishing

Audaciously YOU!

Dedication

To my son, Brandon (Big Wolf): As my first born you've taught me a lot; maybe even more than I've ever taught you. Thank you for showing me how to be bold and resilient in the face of the storm and that true shelter can only be found in the recesses of one's heart. I love you and I am super proud of you!

To my daughter, Lauren: I spent a great deal of my life bold and brave, yet partially visible; and then you came along and showed me that true audacity is intended to cast a light. Thank you for not being afraid to live your dreams and wanting to publish your first book now and doing it. And really, thank you for being Audaciously YOU! And for reminding me that our gifts & talents truly are for all of the world to see and not to be reserved for when we "grow up"!

To my mother, Diana Bond: I never knew a truer warrior until I first saw you. Thank you for helping me to hone my instincts in this world and for showing me how a warrior was supposed to be. I am warrior because you are! Thank you for teaching me to roar!

And last but never least: To the seed of the dream on the inside of me, I shall not, will not, let you down. Grow, Baby, Grow!

Table of Contents

✳ How to Use This Book ✳

"Things should be made as simple as possible, but not any simpler."
~ Albert Einstein

Audaciously YOU! is an affirmational book series designed to help you step into the power of who you are so that you can live your dreams in a bigger, better, bolder way.

This book contains 52 reflections of our highest thoughts and intentions; they are a combination of inspirational quotes, coaching and a boldness boosting affirmation. The quotes are those from some of the most impressive thought leaders of our time. The coaching around the quote is inspired from the true essence of what the quote itself is challenging us to believe. The boldness boosting affirmation serves to contradict the negative beliefs that are a part of our mental blueprint as well as provide you with a tool to tap into your inner-most highest self. Each reflection, in its entire splendor, is intended to remind us that we do believe in ourselves and that we possess everything we need to make our dreams come true.

How Affirmations Work: Affirmations are tools that allow you to create a new reality by speaking new energy into old situations. They allow you to hope with expectation and believe that what you spoke shall come to pass. Although there are varied methods of using affirmations, the best that I have found is for you to speak them aloud while looking yourself eye-to-eye in the mirror. This forces you to acknowledge what you want and to believe you are able to create it. I also recommend stating the affirmations in the morning as soon as you awaken and at night right before you go to sleep. This is because the critical filter of our minds, the part of us that operates as our very own secret service protecting our systems from harm, sleeps when we sleep. This means, information is able to bypass this protective measure and the seeds of that thought are planted with little hope for rejection or removal.

This book is not intended to be read front-to-back and cover-to-cover. It is a tool that you can read however is best suited for you. There are 52 reflections total. This breaks down to one per week. So, do them weekly. Or, feel free to read a reflection per day, a one per week, read it from cover-to-cover, or randomly choose a page for your reading pleasure. The choice is yours! Whichever you choose, this book is definitely geared to provide all that is promised. After reading each reflection, you will have no choice but to boost your boldness and live your biggest dreams.

THE WARRIOR'S CREED:

I AM WARRIOR!

I AM unafraid of becoming

What I AM Purposed to be

Of living the life, I AM destined to live

And engaging in battles to fulfill my destiny.

My methods are rarely, if ever, understood

My specialized maneuvers feared by the common man

I fail to fit in as I have cracked the code

on what it takes to shine and stand.

I weather life's' storms like the hero I AM

And even when I fail, I succeed in my vow

I AM a soldier who came to conquer the world…

And I absolutely refuse to turn back now!

❧ Introduction ❧

Being Audaciously Me

"Your dreams are waiting for you; you just have to have the audacity to believe it."
~ Tonoa Bond

O ne phrase that I have heard all of my life is, "You have the audacity to…" This phrase was uttered, in some way, shape or form, from people who were irritated that I had the nerve to live my life my way without their approval. And regardless to how they finish this sentence, my response, both in word and in deed, has always unequivocally been, "Yes I do!"

It never mattered to me if I was speaking to someone in higher command during my time in the United States Army, if I was acting against my mother's wishes as a highly spirited yet seemingly rebellious teenager, or if I was biding my time in Corporate America expecting the same level of respect from others who thought it their right to demand the ultimate of respect from me. I have always lived by the code of audacity and I refuse to be less than the person I know I AM created to be in order to make another person comfortable around me.

My name, Tonoa, is Samoan. It means, "To command". And when it comes to believing in myself and my dreams, I truly live up to my name. I have always believed it to be my God-given right to be audaciously me. I believe I AM purposed to take the chances this stance inspires and I refuse to allow anyone to take said right away from me. And let me tell you, I have done some pretty audacious things in my life. Some of the things I have done are things that others would never dare. These behaviors are such a part of my story that the moniker of audacity is now a part of my brand.

I am known as "The Audacity Expert", and when I boldly and bravely tell others who I AM, it means something to me. I say these words with pride because I know that without audacity leading the way my dreams are not possible. This name and title expresses to the world that I am willing to take the necessary risks to ensure my dreams and the dreams of those around me come to pass. And it is a title I take great pride in living up to; both for myself and for others. It is my honor to help other Warriors learn the skills necessary to exhibit this same level of pride within themselves.

To be defined as audacious means you possess within you a shameless boldness. It means, you are a person with a high level of contempt for being restrained and that you possess an arrogant disregard for the conventional, "color inside the lines" or "live inside the box" mentality of others. Being audacious means you know who you are, causing others around you to know who you are, because you would not have it any other way.

For the past 8 years, I have gone by the moniker of "The Audacity Expert". From the housing projects of Chicago, to the United States Army, to Corporate America and later into entrepreneurship, I have never allowed another person's beliefs in me or about me - regardless of their rank or station in life - to stop me from believing for myself. And this, coupled with all the education, training and certifications, makes me excellent at what I do. These experiences speak boldly and audaciously on my behalf and remind me to never give up!

My first warrior teacher was my mother. She was that ever constant presence that forced me to never allow my circumstances to win or dictate my beliefs. Growing up in the environment that I did, I had to learn early to fight my way through life. And if I did not fight back, or if I lost said fight, my mother would march me right back to the person or place where the fight occurred and make me fight again. She said it was her job to ensure that I remained strong and that I did not allow the failures in life to make me afraid to live. And I so love and appreciate her for that!

Warrior, we were born audacious. We were born BAD! We are one thousand percent Bold, Audacious, and Determined. The evidence of this exists in the younger version of ourselves. It exists within the inner child in us who jumped from places too high, who put their hands on hot stoves regardless of the shouted warnings, who tasted things that were not meant to be tasted, and did things that were not meant to be done. We did not develop a concept of fear until someone taught us there was something to fear; and even then we fought against that conventional wisdom until we were able to prove it to ourselves.

Yes, it wasn't until we fell off the beds we previously jumped on, until we got burned by the heat of the stove, or got sick from something that really was not meant for human consumption, that we realized there actually was something to fear. For some of us, this did not stop us from wanting to dare. However, for many others; those who allowed their audacity to wane; those who became contented to live inside the boxes that life painted for them; those who did not have warrior mentors as I had in my mom, that fear stopped them from taking the risks necessary to become all they were destined to become.

Audacious people know what their purpose and mission is in life. And us audacious people are so committed to it that we would dare anyone to try and convince us to be anything other than the persons we were created to be. When we operate as our most audacious selves, we are able to live our lives with an air of being fearless and daring. We are inspired to take risks because we know that with every risk we take, regardless of the outcome of said risk, we get one step closer to living the bigger, better, bolder lives our dreams are made of.

So, are you audacious? Do you recognize yourself in any of the above-mentioned definitions? Were you able to pinpoint the exact moments in your life where you could see how these definitions applied to you -- even if they only applied once in-a-while? If you did, congratulations. If you did not, please know this person is within you. This person is within us all.

It doesn't really matter if you have played big and bold in your life and are already operating on a bigger scale than most. Nor does it matter if your audacity is lying dormant, waiting for its opportunity to shine. There is always a bigger playing field to play on and there will always be more to do. The time is always NOW to be merciless in ignoring the beliefs of others. The time is NOW to boldly step out and do those things your Purpose is begging of you. The time is NOW for you to step up to the plate of life and swing for all it's worth. The time is NOW for you to become Audaciously YOU!

This is the purpose for this book. The idea came to me over 20 years ago. My desire, then and now, was to provide a pocket manual to help others see into their innermost parts. It was my hope that a book such as this would provide you with a reflection of the promise of who you could become. And I am honored this book has finally come to fruition. It is my own reflection of 20+ years of thought, feelings and beliefs for helping you to become your most audacious self and to be Audaciously YOU!

It is my hope that this book will remind you to be who you are in every way possible. That you will become aware of both your supporters and your haters. That you will realize that those who believe your bold appeal for a dream-filled life is "overly confident or reckless" are those who really just want to control your destiny. These are people who want to personally construct the lines they need you to color inside so they are comfortable. And this has to stop. I hope that you will use this book, and the audacious contents therein, to step into becoming your most audacious self by refusing to allow others to stop you from living your biggest, brightest and boldest dreams.

Warrior, your Purpose is too big for any box and your destiny is too wild to be restrained. YOU ARE A WARRIOR! You are a brave and experienced soldier fighting to fulfill your destiny and make your Purpose come to light. It is my hope that you will read this book, or the reflections and affirmations that appeal to you most, as often as possible. This will allow your inner child to remind you of who you can be when you allow boldness and audacity to be your guide.

So Warrior, be audacious; be intrepid, be daring and be bold. Make a commitment to live your dreams without shame or regard for the limitations of others! Demand of yourself and others an openness to receive the best that life has to offer! Determine right now today that you are going to be *Audaciously YOU!* And that you refuse to allow anyone to take this birthright away from you.

Because your dreams are waiting for you… you just have to have the audacity to believe it!

Tonoa Bond, MS, PhD(s), MPC, PCPsych, CHt
The Audacity Expert

❧ Reflection 1 ❧

"The first quality that is needed is audacity."

~ Winston Churchill

✗ A WARRIOR'S REFLECTION ✗

When you look at the events, and all of the industrialization that has happened throughout the history of the world, the characteristic that was necessary to make any and all come to pass was that of audacity.

To be audacious means that you possess within you a shameless boldness or an arrogant disregard for conventional thought. Great individuals are not great simply because of the things that they do. Great individuals are great because they carry within their hearts the spirit of audacity and refuse to quit or allow defeat. Audacious people dare to do great things while others are filled with doubt. They leave their marks on the world by standing tall and trudging forward while others are rendered immobile by the voices of fear and their belief in the impossibilities.

The first quality that is needed in each and every endeavor is audacity! Starting today, become shamelessly bold in pursuit of your dreams, hopes and aspirations. Become arrogant in your disregard for the limitations that naysayers would try to place on your life. You were born audacious, and the time has come to raise your head, square your shoulders, and boldly choose to live the life that others would only dare to dream.

✗ A WARRIOR'S AFFIRMATION ✗

I AM bold, audacious and determined. I arrogantly pursue, without fear, all that life has promised to me.

❧ Reflection 2 ❧

"Dreams are as butterflies; cocooned in the soul & destined to fly. What's your dream?"

~ Tonoa Bond

✗ A WARRIOR'S REFLECTION ✗

I believe that butterflies were created to be beautiful reminders of two very important truths; that we were born to be free, and that we are now and always have been destined to fly!

Each and every dream that we possess contains within it the power of flight. And as our dreams sit in wait, nestled within the seat of our souls, they are preparing for the journeys ahead; ready to fly us to heights never before accomplished. As they wait, they are developing the strength necessary to take us on this voyage unencumbered. They are carrying us to the end of our destiny as liberated as a butterfly; encased in the beauty that only our dreams, goals and aspirations can inspire.

So the questions to ask yourself are these: "Am I dreaming or settling?" "Am I flying higher and higher with each and every choice that I make, or am I refusing to awaken to the possibilities, remaining grounded while others around me are experiencing the beauty of flight?"

Freedom is waiting on the other side of your dreams; but you will only experience it when you develop the courage to fly. So take a chance and spread your wings. And when you do, not only will you be living your dreams, but you will also be inspiring others to live theirs as well.

✗ A WARRIOR'S AFFIRMATION ✗

I know that I AM free to fly. I AM ready to reach the magnificent heights of all that life has to offer.

✎ Reflection 3 ✎

"I have not failed. I've just found 10,000 ways
that won't work."

~ Thomas Edison

✗ A WARRIOR'S REFLECTION ✗

Thomas Edison is on record as having more failures under his belt than most people have tries under theirs. He failed over 10,000 times with every patent he'd ever attempted before finally achieving success with the light bulb. TEN THOUSAND TIMES. And for this reason alone he should be heralded as the definition of persistence. Because even in the face of insane failure, he was not afraid to continue forth with determined and unrelenting action. What he knew, that others did not, was that beyond a shadow of a doubt, with every patent he submitted, he was one step closer to making his dreams come true.

I'm sure it's easy to judge Edison's actions as insane, because nobody has that kind of determination, right? Often times, having it all requires that you push forward even when the circumstances look bleak. Don't you think that your dreams are worth it? Don't you want to experience the true essence of your destiny?

Stop limiting yourself and your success by giving yourself an out. No matter how long you have been on this path, your dreams are worth the extra effort. And in order for you to tap into your greatness so that you can finally succeed, you just might have to try, and try, and try again.

Edison did it 10,000 times, and had he quit we might still be sitting in the dark today. Can't you take a chance and try at least a few more times so that you can live your dreams as well? If at first you don't succeed… well, eventually you will, so go ahead and try, and try and try again!

✗ A WARRIOR'S AFFIRMATION ✗

I AM energized to continue to pursue my dreams. I AM now determined to succeed and have become unstoppable

೬ Reflection 4 ೩

"There are no limits for those who don't know
they exist."

~ Joyal Mehta

✗ A WARRIOR'S REFLECTION ✗

There is so much that we can learn from toddlers. They were born into a fearless existence and know deep down that as human beings, placed here on this earth for a specific purpose, we were born to be free.

Toddlers are not afraid to challenge their potential and take the chances necessary to see what awaits them on the other side of the moment. And even though adults may judge their movements to be reckless and dangerous, what they are teaching those of us willing to pay attention and learn is that there really are no limits, except for those that we accept and place on ourselves.

Webster defines the word "limit" as something that bounds, restrains or confines. Not a warm and fuzzy kind of definition is it? Yet, so many of us allow ourselves to become warm and fuzzy with life's limitations. Why? Because it is easier to comply and be bound within the confines of our comfort zones than it is to step into our potential and be free.

Audacious Warrior, you were born with limitless potential. This means you have within you an inherent, unstoppable capacity for coming into being. And whatever this being is supposed to be cannot be capped! So, are you still on the road to becoming or are you your own worst enemy; limiting your potential and placing restrictions on your dreams?

To be or not to be, this really is the question... But more important than the question is... what's your answer going to be?

✗ A WARRIOR'S AFFIRMATION ✗

I AM unstoppable! My potential is limitless! And I AM taking my dreams by storm!

❧ **Reflection 5** ☙

"When someone says they are having a bad day
I always say, "compared to what?"

~ Unknown

✗ A WARRIOR'S REFLECTION ✗

The Law of Polarity states that everything has two polarities oppositions, or extremes - and whenever one extreme is present, the opposite of it has to be present as well. If there is good, there has to be bad. If there is right, there has to be wrong. And so on and so on. However, it's like two sides of a coin; while heads and tails exist on said coin, you cannot see them both at the same time. In that same manner, in order to make either polarity present in your life, you have to flip the coin.

The true power of this Universal Law is that nothing has meaning or value in your life until you assign it meaning and value. No experience can be classified or ranked in your life or belief system until you decide to place it on the scale and judge it based on our past experiences. So a day is just a day, and an experience is just an experience, until you weigh it based on other events or experiences in your life that fit the same criteria.

Nothing is good or bad, nothing is right or wrong, and nothing is black or white. What they each are is polarity; they are words that when said cause emotional reactions forcing you to judge every experience as the same. However, now is the time to change the lens that you use to see that world. Now is the time for you to release the need to argue for your limitations and get on the road to living the audacious life that your dreams are made of.

No matter what your prior experiences have been, a day really is just a day and a moment really is just a moment; nothing more, nothing less. But if it doesn't feel this way, then flip a coin. In the action of that moment, you will see that the choice really is yours!

✗ A WARRIOR'S AFFIRMATION ✗

I choose to release any and all negative thoughts about my day. I see my life through the lens of positivity. All is good and it is well.

15

❧ **Reflection 6** ❧

"I was always looking outside myself for strength and confidence but it comes from within. It is there all the time."

~ Anna Freud

✗ A WARRIOR'S REFLECTION ✗

It is actually a huge misnomer that strength and confidence are traits that have to be developed. The truth of the matter is that we were all born with a healthy dose of both. However, what does need to be developed is our readiness to use them when needed.

Webster defines confidence as a belief in one's abilities or an assurance that you can do that which you have set out to do. So how does one believe they are confident or develop the assurance they have what they need to be successful? Through preparation and practice -- readying yourself to successfully face those situations in life that call for you to step up to the plate and give it your all.

It is by mirroring the actions of others who are successful, as well as by remembering those times in your past where you were strong and confident, that you will create a template to follow in order to have even more such times in the future. It is then that you will no longer need to feel as if the weight of the world is on your shoulders. You will know that you know that you know that you have what it takes to be successful.

Strength and confidence are already on the inside of you. All you have to do to make them visible is believe it. And once you believe it, you will then have no other choice but to be it.

✗ A WARRIOR'S AFFIRMATION ✗

I AM worthy of the highest vision that I hold for my life. I AM confident that all of my dreams will happen for me starting today.

17

✎ **Reflection 7** ✎

"There came a time when the risk to remain tight in the bud was more painful than the risk to blossom."

~ Anaïs Nin

✗ A WARRIOR'S REFLECTION ✗

Have you ever slept on your arm the wrong way, or had your legs elevated or tucked under for too long and felt the pin needles of numbness radiating through you?

What this tingling feeling signifies is that you are in the process of starving said body part of oxygen; and a prolonged deprivation of oxygenated blood could cause the tissues in this area of your body to die. Translation -- if the situation is not rectified in a timely manner you could quite possibly cause some irrevocable damage to that limb or body part for good.

Now pay attention to your life and your Purpose. Can you recognize these same signs in your life where your dreams are concerned? Do you feel this tingling feeling deep within some abandoned goal begging for you to breathe life into it? Do you realize your dream is begging for a release from its imprisonment so it can blossom and be all it is destined to be?

Don't become an amputee on the path to fulfilling your Purpose. Stop restricting the blood flow to your dreams. Life is calling for you to water those seeds of greatness so you can bloom into the most fragrant flower this life has ever seen. The most painful part of death is knowing that you are dying and have yet to live. Take the risk. Open up! You won't regret it!

✗ A WARRIOR'S AFFIRMATION ✗

I AM stepping out in faith that the world is ready for my gifts. I AM open! I AM alive! I AM free!

❧ Reflection 8 ❧

"There is one thing stronger than all the armies of the world, and that is an idea whose time has come."

~ Victor Hugo

⚔ A WARRIOR'S REFLECTION ⚔

How many times have you seen an invention in a store or heard someone's idea brought to life on television and thought to yourself, "That should have been me!"

An idea is a gift of creation. It is born on the wings of a butterfly waiting for its chance to soar. It is defined as the main thing that you are thinking about; your intention or that which you intend to do. This means that once the thought enters into your conscious awareness, it carries within it the possibilities for existence and only needs your skills, gifts and talents to make it come to pass. And because all ideas are energy, and the same energy is available to all, it is definitely possible for someone else to snatch them from the stream of Universal Consciousness and bring them to life before you ever have a chance.

Just like you, your ideas have within them seeds of actualizing potential. This means that every idea comes with the power it needs to unleash its greatness to the world. All you need to do to water this seed is believe in its potential; to do the legwork necessary and watch as it comes to pass.

What ideas are ruminating in your mind waiting for you to inhale the breath of belief in order to make them come true? Get to work already! Your time has come! And both you, and the idea brewing inside of you, know it. Because really, how many more times in your life do you want to hear yourself utter the words, "Hey, that should have been me?"

⚔ A WARRIOR'S AFFIRMATION ⚔

I AM ideas brought to life. I honor intention in my life and create all that I have been destined to create.

21

❧ Reflection 9 ❧

"We confide in our strength, without boasting
of it, we respect that of others, without fearing
it."

~ Thomas Jefferson

✗ A WARRIOR'S REFLECTION ✗

Quite often people confuse strength with power and spend a great deal of their lives trampling on those who appear to be weak in hopes of making themselves appear strong. They believe that when others fear them this makes them powerful. And being the power hungry vampires they are, they use hurtful words or degrading phrases in order to ruin the lives of others in an attempt to stop them from being powerful in their own right.

However, when you look at what behaviors such as these mean, you begin to see that all this person is really proving is that they are insecure. They are confused about their own mission in life and recognize in others what they are unable to recognize in themselves... what true confidence and success looks like.

The only person who has any real power in your life is you. And you are such a powerful person that you never have to live in fear that another person's power or vision will outshine your own. So, ask yourself, "Who really holds the power in my life? And am I willing to be bigger, better, and bolder in my life from this point forward?"

Remember, it is when you remain confident and pursue your dreams in the cloak of your own power that you will surely have the admiration and respect of others -- and more importantly, you will have the admiration and respect of yourself.

✗ A WARRIOR'S AFFIRMATION ✗

I choose today to never fear another because of who they are. I AM strong and I AM mentally capable of creating the life that I desire.

❧ Reflection 10 ❧

"Our greatest glory is not in never failing, but in rising up every time we fail."

~ Ralph Waldo Emerson

✗ A WARRIOR'S REFLECTION ✗

The criterion for failure is usually judged through the experiences that we allow to shape our lives. But just because we fall down while travelling on the road of success does not mean that we have failed; sometimes it simply means we need the help or assistance of another to pull us up and help us achieve our goals.

True failure is not in the falling down but in the staying down. And it becomes a moot point that's null and void the moment you get back up. If you are classifying an event or action in your life as a failure, this does not mean that you are out for the count. However, what it can mean is that you need some help at this venture in your life.

Asking for help is not a sign of weakness. It's actually a sign of strength. It helps you find a way to quickly align with others who are travelling along the same path. It also helps you not to feel so alone. And the help you ask for does not have to be for something big. You can make it a simple request or an elaborate one... the most important thing – to help you transcend your current moment and embrace you new one – is that you step fully into your boldness and ask.

No one ever makes it in this world alone. So step outside of your comfort zone and embrace your glory. And if you need someone to have your back just ask, because you never know what the answer might be and where a little help from a friend can lead you.

✗ A WARRIOR'S AFFIRMATION ✗

I gladly ask for assistance from others. I know that the road to completing my goals and living my dreams happens faster when I AM open to allowing the help of others into my life.

❧ Reflection 11 ☙

"The question isn't who is going to let me; it's who is going to stop me?"

~ Ayn Rand

⚔ A WARRIOR'S REFLECTION ⚔

How many times in your life have you told someone something that you wanted to do, be or accomplish and they tried to talk you out of it with words of gloom and doom, doubt and despair? Or worse, they sought to belittle your dreams in hopes of making you feel small and unaccomplished, leaving you without a hope or prayer of making said dreams come true?

So many people in our lives believe that we need their permission in order to be great or to do great things. And if they don't give us said permission and we go on to do great things anyway, they try to convince us that we will fail so that we give up our dreams and live a life of the same miserable commonality that they too are suffering. And as much as they know they were born to have more, many give up their dreams because it's easier to give in than it is to take a stand for what they want or to fight for what they believe in.

Don't allow this to be you. You are the most powerful person in the world and you have been destined to complete the tasks that only you can complete. It would be a shame to allow anyone, including yourself, to tell you otherwise. You do not need anyone's permission to be great! And, knowing what I know about you and your destiny, even if others do believe that you need their permission to be great or to do great things, they should be hard-pressed to try and stop you.

⚔ A WARRIOR'S AFFIRMATION ⚔

I know that I AM powerful beyond measure. I refuse to seek the approval of another or to allow anyone to stop me from being great and living my dreams!

27

❧ **Reflection 12** ☙

"Boldness has genius, power, and magic in it.
Begin it now."

~ Johann Wolfgang von Goethe

⚔ A WARRIOR'S REFLECTION ⚔

If there is one thing in life that we can be absolutely certain of, it is that many people are in awe of the bold. Why? Because the bold refuse to fit in while the onlookers of life – those who are afraid to step into their greatness and live their dreams – have allowed society to convince them that it is wrong to stand out. So for them, observing those of us who are audacious and bold is an experience. But instead of seeking to have this experience for themselves, they'd prefer to grab some popcorn, sit on the sidelines and watch as their lives pass them by.

To those who are afraid to stand out and be different, we resemble mythical creatures, or some never before seen being. Watching us, they cannot help but to sit in awe of our character and wonder what it would be like to step outside of their carefully painted boxes and become us -- even if just for a moment.

Aren't you ready to live out your genius? Don't you want to step into your power? Isn't your life begging you for a sprinkle of magic? There is genius, power and magic in you and you show it every time you reveal to the world who you really are. So step out and be bold because the world is watching… might as well give them something to look at.

⚔ A WARRIOR'S AFFIRMATION ⚔

I AM comfortable stepping out and showing the world who I AM. I refuse to fit in and I stand firm in my determination to unapologetically stand out.

৯ **Reflection 13** ৶

"Mirrors should think longer before they reflect."

~Jean Cocteau

✗ A WARRIOR'S REFLECTION ✗

The scientific Law of Reflection states that when an object bounces off of a flat surface, the angle at which it hits the surface will be equal to the angle at which it bounces away, thus creating a reflection.

When we look at this metaphysically, we can see that we were created to be mirrors of one another in order for us to see in ourselves that which we would never see otherwise. That every person, or event, shows up in our lives as an honest and accurate reflection of our deepest secrets and as a representation of the persons we truly are. This means, whenever we interact with another, whether we like said person or not, we are seeing something in them that is reflected within ourselves.

With this in mind, we should take to heart the words of Cocteau when we are tempted to project our views onto another. We should remember to think long and hard before we judge them, remembering to treat them with the same level of respect and empathy we would want them to have with us. Because at the end of the day, we can only see in them that which we truly are; which means, the only person we are truly judging is ourselves.

✗ A WARRIOR'S AFFIRMATION ✗

I AM a reflection of all that I value in the Universe. I mirror the change that I want to see in my world.

❧ Reflection 14 ❧

"The important thing is not to stop questioning. Curiosity has its own reason for existing."

~ Albert Einstein

✕ A WARRIOR'S REFLECTION ✕

A question is defined as something that is waiting for an answer, and often times this applies to our lives as well.

When we are not as focused on our purpose as we should be, or when we fail to embrace our curiosity, we spend many wasted days living under the guise of intention; pretending to be living our dreams when we are not even sure what said dream means to us. Our lives are sitting in limbo waiting for an answer, when in all honesty, we have already forgotten the question.

To become all we are intended to be, we are supposed to challenge the questions & question the challenges? Life has presented to us a specific problem. We need to embrace our curiosity so that we can challenge the answer we are currently providing in order to find the proper answer that will move our lives forward.

As Richard Feynman once stated, "There is no learning without having to pose a question." So never stop asking questions; because it is in the answers that you find the seeds for your growth. And never be afraid to challenge another person's perspective; because it is in the answers provided that they will receive the tools needed to help them grow.

The most important thing for you to remember today is that life is asking you a question... are you finally ready to give it an answer?

✕ A WARRIOR'S AFFIRMATION ✕

I AM open to learning and growing. I choose today to be open to curiosity so I can answer the questions which govern my life.

✌ **Reflection 15** ❧

"No matter what you are experiencing in your life right now, your dream is always bigger than the moment."

~ Tonoa Bond

⚔ A WARRIOR'S REFLECTION ⚔

We have all had moments in our lives, big or small, where it seemed that nothing was working out the way we wanted it to. Where it seemed as if life was intended on teaching us one big lesson, all at once, and there was nothing we could do but to brace ourselves and suck it up.

Life is life, and boy, does it not play fair. However, the best thing to remember is that no matter what hurricanes have swept through your life leaving destruction and devastation, no matter the black hole that has seemingly sucked your life into its never-ending void, your dream, your purpose, your destiny – whatever it is you call that which you were created it to be – is now and will always be bigger than the moment.

No matter what you are experiencing at this moment in time, the seed of potential on the inside OF you is bigger than anything that is happening TO you! There is so much more to your life than this mere moment in time. And if you keep this in mind, and have the AUDACITY to believe that your purpose is bigger than your pain, and your destiny is bigger than your now, then when your outward pain tries to silence your inward potential, you will be infused with the necessary strength to be the unstoppable being you were created to be.

You are destined for greatness. Now is the time to activate your Audacity Quotient™ and boldly move in the direction of your dreams! The moments might be painful, but they should never win; because who you are and will continue to become is now and always will be bigger than any and every moment.

⚔ A WARRIOR'S AFFIRMATION ⚔

The purpose for my life is so much bigger than this moment in time.
I AM audaciously moving forward with my dreams refusing to allow
anything or anyone to stop me.

❧ Reflection 16 ❧

"You may delay, but time will not."

~ Benjamin Franklin

✗ A WARRIOR'S REFLECTION ✗

Time is the only equator amongst men. Just like the Law of Gravity, the construct of time is no respecter of persons. No matter who a person is, or how seemingly successful or well-known they are, every human being only get 24-hours in a day -- nothing more, nothing less. The only difference that exists between those who do extraordinary things with their time and those who do not is how they choose to use it.

Successful people maximize their time to the nth degree. Meaning, they make sure that every minute of their day is scheduled with activity that will move their dreams and goals forward. And rarely do they deviate from that plan. Do you think the Bill Gates and Oprah's of the world are making excuses about how they spend their time? No, because they know they are supposed to spend it wisely. They would not be where they are, in the top 1% of successful people in the world, if they did anything less.

Excuses or not, time will not wait for you to "get it together". It will continue to pass along, at the same rate, whether you're ready for it to pass or not. So, set your goals, create a plan, and invest your time wisely. Because, in doing so, you will both achieve and reap maximum results in your life. And these types of results will move you forward at a speed you couldn't have dared to even dream about.

✗ A WARRIOR'S AFFIRMATION ✗

My time is scheduled wisely. I AM working my plan and achieving success in every area of my life.

✎ Reflection 17 ✎

"Most of the important things in the world have been accomplished by people who have kept on trying when there seemed to be no hope at all."

~ Dale Carnegie

✗ A WARRIOR'S REFLECTION ✗

One thing that we should stop telling others is "There is a great big world out there" if we are not going to show them how they fit in it. What many people attribute to a loss of hope is nothing more than fit; knowing who you are, what you want and where you belong. It is in knowing these specific answers that we have the strength and courage to persevere in our toughest challenges.

When we doubt our place in the world, it is easy to live beneath our purpose. It is easy to believe that it is okay to give up and waste precious time on earth by settling for the crumbs we are offered when the whole pie is already ours.

There is now, and always will be, hope for you. You have a valid and valuable contribution to make to this world. Whether you have accomplished more than most people seemingly ever will or if you are still wondering where to begin, you have a demand on your life to keep moving forward until your last breath leaves your body. So get up, brush yourself off, and grab life by the bootstraps; because you have work to do. And I AM too selfish to allow you to quit. Greatness inspires greatness; and someone in this world needs your example of the greatness you are to show them just how great they too can actually be.

✗ A WARRIOR'S AFFIRMATION ✗

I AM an example to myself and to others of what can be
accomplished when I acknowledge my place in this world. My future
is bright and greatness is within me!

❧ **Reflection 18** ❧

"Don't be afraid to give up the good to go for the great."

~ John D. Rockefeller

✗ A WARRIOR'S REFLECTION ✗

Many people waste precious time and resources attempting to do those things that were not intended for them while letting their own gifts and talents fall by the wayside. They find themselves in competition with the gifts and talents of others determined to prove that they are better; not realizing the task they are focused on fulfilling is not their dream. And quite frankly, it is not something they should be investing their time in anyway.

Because we were created with an abundant survival mentality, we are smart and resourceful beings who have the ability to be and do whatever it is that we set our minds to. However, just because we can do something does not mean that we should. Because even though there are tons of things we are good at, there is only one purpose that we have been created for. What keeps us stuck in this unproductive rut is the fear of the unknown; it guides us off the path that leads to our dreams and leaves us feeling empty and frustrated.

Just because you are good at something does not mean it is meant for your focus. You have been neurologically gifted to fulfill a specific purpose and your gifts are unique to you and you alone. So, spend your time fulfilling those purposes you have been created for and leave the rest for those to whom they have been specifically designed. Because, if it hasn't been created for you, you shouldn't want it anyway. And most importantly, you have to be willing to sacrifice those things of which you are simply good in order to ever have and become that which is definitively great!

✗ A WARRIOR'S AFFIRMATION ✗

I welcome new opportunities and resources. I boldly live the great life I AM destined to live.

⤳ **Reflection 19** ⤳

"There is nothing in a caterpillar that tells you
it's going to be a butterfly."

~ Richard Buckminster Fuller

✗ A WARRIOR'S REFLECTION ✗

Butterflies are one of the best examples of the transformational beauty within us all. When you look at their overall life journey, what you can see is that no matter what mistakes you have made or how unattractive your journey has been, there is still hope for the beauty in your life to shine through.

Think about their beginning. The disproportionate body and overall plumpness of a caterpillar so does not scream grace, beauty, or winged flight. It's fat, clunky and it leaves unattractive deposits of shed skin everywhere it goes. However, the caterpillar knows that it's working on something big – even if it does not quite know what it is.

The caterpillar knows that while its journey seems impossible to most, what awaits him is so great that it has to follow along with its course of action, regardless of what the rest of the world might think or believe. It knows beyond a shadow of a doubt that even in the ugliness of it all it is standing in the beauty of the moment, and for him this is all that matters.

What are you working on? When you look at your life, are you sitting in your cocoon of greatness transforming into that which you were intended to be, or are you wallowing in your sorrow refusing to do what is necessary to make your dreams come true? Choose today to stand in the seed of your purpose -- because regardless of what the rest of the world believes is possible for you, it is time for you to believe that just like the fat, clunky, graceless caterpillar, you too can fly!

✗ A WARRIOR'S AFFIRMATION ✗

I have the audacity to believe that I AM working on something big. I know that all of my former days of hurt and pain were worth it.

❧ Reflection 20 ❧

"You can easily judge the character of a man by how he treats those who can do nothing for him."

~ Johann Wolfgang von Goethe

✗ A WARRIOR'S REFLECTION ✗

Evolutionary psychology tells us that we were born to survive in groups and that it was in the helping, learning from, and caring for our fellow man that we were able to grow, progress and evolve.

However, as the human condition continued to advance, we seemingly became a world of overly "me" conscious individuals. We became so afraid of the possibilities of lack and limitation that we no longer act on our first instinct to offer assistance to those in need. And even if we do offer to assist "them" in some way, it's usually not from the heart. We do so with the expectation that they will owe us something in return -- and boy oh boy do we make sure to collect.

The word character from the Greek means "engraved" or "stamped/branding mark." When others look at you, what are they seeing branded on your person? Is this brand or symbol something that resembles the true nature of who you really are? Is fear, or some other form of negativity, engraved in your heart and controlling your life? Do not allow fear to stop you from being a person of integrity or character. Reach out to assist others in need, without fear. You were born for this moment; to be "their" hero in this moment of space and time. So ask yourself, do you really want to allow these moments to pass you by?

✗ A WARRIOR'S AFFIRMATION ✗

I AM branded with the mark of excellence. I act on my first instinct to help others in need because I recognize the beauty and strength in putting others first.

❧ **Reflection 21** ❧

"Nobody can make you feel inferior without
your consent."

~ Eleanor Roosevelt

✘ A WARRIOR'S REFLECTION ✘

When looking at this quote by Roosevelt, the rational minded person within us should wonder why one would ever consent to feeling inferior at the hands of another. What is it that another person could ever say that would cause us to accept their judgments of us. What words from their mouths would we allow to hit our spirits in such a way that would cause us to refuse to see what's good and special within ourselves?

Consent in this manner means you have given your permission, approval or agreement to another to determine your beliefs about yourself. According to the Laws of Belief Formation, we have been created to comprehend, and to believe to be true, every proposition that is given to us. However, after hearing said proposition, it is then up to us to utilize rational thought to decide whether or not we should <u>dis</u>-believe said proposition and see ourselves as different than that which has been stated and believed. This means it is in the believing, and the continued believing, of what others say about us that grant them unfettered consent to make us feel about ourselves however they want us to feel.

Never allow what another person says about you to cause you to feel anything less than the beautiful, brilliant person that you are. Do the work to <u>dis</u>-believe their propositions and never, ever, give your consent to believe yourself as anything less than the person who you were created to be.

✘ A WARRIOR'S AFFIRMATION ✘

I AM the person I desire to be. I know who I AM and will continue to be that which I was created to be.

❧ Reflection 22 ❦

"None are so poor that they have nothing to give... and none are so rich that they have nothing to receive."

~ John Paul II

✗ A WARRIOR'S REFLECTION ✗

Giving and receiving are always subjected to forms of prejudice and internal bias at the highest levels. We tend to allow giving or receiving in our own lives based on the judgments we have for or against the person to whom we want to either give to or receive from. If we see ourselves as better than said person, then we give down but will not allow them to gift up; and if we believe ourselves lowly or in desperate need then we will take another's gifts while never believing it to be possible that we have something to offer them in return.

When you allow this glass ceiling type thinking in your life, you unknowingly place invisible barriers on who can assist you and you place limitations on exactly what it is you have to offer. This selfishness hinders the advancement of the human condition leaving you collectively un-evolved and stuck in the muck and mire of where you currently are in your life.

Challenge yourself to remove the barriers in your life where giving and receiving are concerned and allow life to provide you with what you need to break through the glass ceiling and move to the next level. Because as long as there are others out there looking to live their dreams you will always have something to give. And regardless of how much you have accomplished in your life, there is always a next level so there is something for you to open your hands to receive.

✗ A WARRIOR'S AFFIRMATION ✗

I AM open to the gifts of the Universe. I give and receive with an open heart and a receptive spirit.

℘ **Reflection 23** ๙

"I do my own thing and you do your thing. I'm not in this world to live up to your expectations, and you are not in this world to live up to mine. You are you and I am I."

~ Fritz Perls

✕ A WARRIOR'S REFLECTION ✕

We as a society are participating in a gross misunderstanding of the meaning of the word expectation. And this is mainly because we have forgotten how to expect the best in life. We have cloned ourselves to fall in line with the strong beliefs of what others believe may happen and have ignored our own. Mainly because we believe that in doing so we are somehow making things easier for ourselves.

It's time for you to say YES to individuality? To be an individual means that you possess distinct qualities or characteristics that serve to distinguish you from another person or thing. It means you are willing to take a stand and walk to the beat of your own drum because you know that you have more to offer the world as an individual than you do as a replica of someone else. And because of this, you stand in your own power and base your expectations on what you believe you should receive and not based on someone else's standards.

Stop giving your power away! There is room for all of us to have what we want in this life without needing to yield to another person's expectations. You have to decide today to live up to the responsibility to be the best you that you can be, because it is solely the responsibility of others to do the same for themselves. And never give way to the expectations of another and forget your own; because the minute you do, you metaphorically cease to exist.

✕ A WARRIOR'S AFFIRMATION ✕

I AM the best me that I can be. I only expect of others that which I expect of myself.

❧ Reflection 24 ❧

"A candle loses nothing by lighting another candle."

~ Proverb

✖ A WARRIOR'S REFLECTION ✖

If you look at your life as a conscious observer, can you see the times you were afraid to assist someone else because of your own fear that giving something away meant that you are losing something in the process?

Well, what if you looked at this from a different perspective? What if you realized that the beauty in lighting another person's candle and sharing your light with someone else actually afforded you the opportunity to define your legacy and leave your mark on the world? See, when you put it like that, don't you feel inspired to want to give of yourself freely and more often?

If we were to be selfish and only consider ourselves for a moment, we would see that lighting another's fire, and helping them share their gifts with the world, actually helps to save our own legacy from extinction. At some point, your internal flame will meet its timely demise. However, if your flame has lit, touched and inspired another's then it shall continue forth forever. And as long as this process continues, of the flame you lit lighting and inspiring another, and so on and so forth, your name shall live on forever, leaving an inextinguishable light for the world to continuously reflect.

Giving and receiving are reciprocal; you cannot have one without the other. If your hand and your heart are closed and you're afraid to let go of what you have, how will you receive the abundant blessings that have been set aside for you? For it is only the open hand and the open heart that receive -- and they do this in the same way in which they give (so open your hands already! The entire world is waiting to bless you!).

✖ A WARRIOR'S AFFIRMATION ✖

My hand and my heart are open. I know that what I AM seeking is also seeking me.

✦ **Reflection 25** ✦

"If you are unsure of a course of action, do not attempt it. Your doubts and hesitations will infect your execution. Timidity is dangerous: Better to enter with boldness. Any mistakes you commit through audacity are easily corrected with more audacity. Everyone admires the bold; no one honors the timid."

~ Robert Greene

✗ A WARRIOR'S REFLECTION ✗

General Patton is considered to be one of the most feared military leaders of all time. He is remembered as an eccentric leader who was well known for his commanding leadership and controversial outspokenness. He defeated his enemies because his tactics were considered daring and unpredictable. And he left them cowering in fear because he entered every situation with boldness and mystery leaving them wondering how and when he would attack.

What Patton knew and used to his advantage was that audacity and action are hesitation's enemy. He used each and every moment that called for him to be bold to his advantage. And this is the very reason that Patton is still talked about today; because he was unpredictable and bold.

"Everyone admires the bold." And boldness is why Patton's legacy will continue to stand. He provided us all with a shining example of how to act when war is raging against your dreams, hopes and aspirations. He is sending forth a challenge from the grave for you to step fully into your boldness and become Audaciously YOU!

When you stand toe-to-toe with your fears and you hear the voices of doubt daring to interrupt your progress, live by Patton's example. Live life with no excuses. Boldly pursue your destiny without hesitation. Remind yourself of who you are and what you have accomplished, and boldly step out to accomplish more. Because just as General Patton knew, with a little boldness and audacity on your side, you can have, be and do anything you want!

✗ A WARRIOR'S AFFIRMATION ✗

Today I move with a sense of urgency. I know that I AM the bold one… I AM the bold one… I AM the bold one!

❧ Reflection 26 ❦

"The permission you need to live your dreams
is already yours."

~ Tonoa Bond

✗ A WARRIOR'S REFLECTION ✗

The key to making your dreams come true lies in realizing this key principle: That you don't just have a dream, you are the dream. You were born the dream. You were born the passion, the purpose, and the intention for your life. The skin that covers your body is not the real you – it is just a layer that protects the most important part of who you are... the real you – which is the dream.

The word permission is defined as: "Officially allowing someone to do a particular thing." Waiting for permission from someone else means you do not recognize yourself as the authority figure in your own life. It means you need someone else to tell you that your dream is valid in order for you to be audacious enough to believe it.

Let me tell you this; the permission you need to live your dreams is already yours. Your dream is already alive on the inside of you. All you need to assert this promise into your life is to release the activation principle of your beliefs and expect for that which you desire and are Purposed for to come true.

Decide today that you will not waste another moment waiting for the approval or permission of someone else before moving forward and claiming your destiny. Believe that you can have everything you have ever wanted. And demand that it comes to pass. Because the permission you seek was granted the moment you were born. The dream is already yours. Go ahead and take it!

✗ A WARRIOR'S AFFIRMATION ✗

I AM the dream! Today I release myself from the bondage of others and boldly move forward to bring to life every dream that lives on the inside of me.

❧ **Reflection 27** ☙

"Can you imagine what I would do if I could
do all that I can?"

~ Sun Tzu

✗ A WARRIOR'S REFLECTION ✗

Many of us have lost touch with our imaginations; the part of ourselves that is the creativity center of our dreams. The place that took our younger selves on many magical journeys leading us to experience those visions and dreams we had never experienced before, yet wanted to experience again and again.

Imagination is the place that shows us our dreams are possible. It is the place that shows us all the things we have yet to create. Yet we 'grow up' and are socialized to place that part of ourselves on a shelf. We're told our imaginations are "child's play" and not for adults. But, how can we expect to live our dreams if we've never seen them? And how can we be expected to live our lives on the wings of unlimited possibilities if we can't imagine said possibilities exist?

Imagination is not just for children; it is for all of us. We are to call out to our inner child and allow him or her to hold our hands, create our paths, and lead us to our dreams. We are to ignore any and all thoughts of lack and limitation and live only within the realm of unlimited possibilities because we know for sure they already exist. Your inner child is asking you to let him out to play. They know the way to your dreams and want to help you get there.

So, can you imagine what you would do if you did all that you can? Let's let your inner child answer that question for you. Because I am certain the answer will unabashedly be 'YES'!

✗ A WARRIOR'S AFFIRMATION ✗

I AM the creator of my life and the inventor of my dreams. I know that I AM talented and believe beyond a shadow of a doubt that my dreams are possible.

ᔰ **Reflection 28** ᔱ

"If you would be a real seeker after truth, you must at least once in your life doubt, as far as possible, all things."

~ Descartes

✗ A WARRIOR'S REFLECTION ✗

Universal law tells us that nothing changes until it becomes what it is. And it does not become what it is until we define it in our minds.

Our lives are defined by our constructs; the meanings and interpretations that we place on the events that happen in and to us. But just because we have internally constructed a meaning for an event does not mean that what we have constructed is true. We all interpret reality in myriad ways; not by the facts of what has happened, but rather by what we tell ourselves has happened. And because we are in control of what we believe, we are highly capable of changing our view of the world at any time by simply changing the various meaning we have assigned to it.

You are not a victim of your circumstances; however, you could be a victim of your constructs – the lines you allow your life to live within. Your life is also not dictated by your conditions, but by how you choose to interpret the events that created said conditions.

So, if you don't like the world you're currently living in, change it. Do this by looking at your life and changing the parts of your truth that no longer serve you. It really is that simple. Because until you can stand toe to toe with your reality, see the truth of who you are and change the meanings you have assigned to the events in your life, then nothing in your life is ever going to change.

✗ A WARRIOR'S AFFIRMATION ✗

I AM open to learning new things that will help me to frame my life and construct my truth. I inspire change and I AM open to the possibilities that exist.

✎ **Reflection 29** ✎

"It's not what you look at, it's what you see."

~ Henry David Thoreau

⚔ A WARRIOR'S REFLECTION ⚔

It has been said that one of the greatest paradoxes of our physical senses is that our eyes actually show us what we believe and not what we see. What this means is that we only see things the way that we've been conditioned to see them or as they relate to our stories. It's actually the work of self-preservation; our mind blocks out all of the extra sensory sensation and only takes in the things that contextually fit what we already know.

Since the moment we were born, we have been taking in and storing information from every event and situation that has happened in our lives. This information becomes our stories. It forms the foundations for which we build our lives upon and the lenses in which we see the world. We use said stories to repeatedly tell us who we are and how we fit in said world. So depending on your story, when someone says one thing, you might hear something else, or when someone shows you one thing you may see something totally different; whether it was actually there or not!

So… Are you standing in the background afraid to step into your boldness because of a past hurt or pain? Are you judging everyone by the same measure of the person or people who hurt you? What is it that you believe about yourself and your place in the world? Is this belief valid?

You are the one in control of your life. And if you need to regain said control, simply change the lens in which you see the world. Because, until you take control of your story and change the things that you see, you will never have any idea of all the great things that are possible for your life.

⚔ A WARRIOR'S AFFIRMATION ⚔

I now release myself from the judgment of my past. I AM in control of my life. I now see myself as who I AM destined to be.

63

✎ Reflection 30 ✎

"It is never too late to be what you might have been."

~ George Eliot

⚔ A WARRIOR'S REFLECTION ⚔

Many of us have erroneously allowed the fear of not having enough time to play a role in how we live our lives. And depending on how much or how little time we believe we have left, we tend to hinder our own paths for growth; believing that our time to become whatever it is we really want to be has passed and it is too late to do anything about it.

The great Michelangelo was 71 when he painted the Sistine Chapel. His determination to achieve greatness at this age speaks to his understanding that the time for action is always NOW! Because wouldn't you rather age while on the road to living your dreams than to age anyway having nothing to show for it?

A client once asked me if they should go back to school to get their Master's and PhD as they wouldn't complete said degrees until they were 55. My response was, "You're going to turn 55 anyway, right? So the true question is, would you rather be 55 with your degree or without it?" This slight shift in perspective led them to an "aha" moment. It helped them decide to move forward with their life and to begin to fulfill that dream.

Time does not have a right to dictate to you what you can or cannot become. The only way it will ever be too late for you is if you never begin. So get to it already -- no more stalling. The world is waiting for your gifts.

⚔ A WARRIOR'S AFFIRMATION ⚔

I AM unstoppable and invest my time wisely. There are no limits to who I will become.

✛ **Reflection 31** ✛

"When I dare to be powerful, to use my strength in the service of my vision, then it becomes less and less important whether I am afraid."

~ Audre Lorde

✗ A WARRIOR'S REFLECTION ✗

Fear is actually a conditioned response. Growing up, many of us were surrounded by limitations; whether real or imagined, whether imposed upon us by others or self-imposed. The minute we spoke our dreams to certain people in our lives they spoke fear, doubt and lack over them. Their fear and non-belief spread until it wore us down and began to believe that living in a world of mediocrity, lack and limitations was all we were capable of.

The fear of failure is a lie that many have unfortunately accepted. In this acceptance, it becomes easy for one to believe in their limitations instead of stepping out of the box and into their most powerful selves. And what is it that we're really afraid of? In a nutshell... succeeding.

If we were to actually succeed at all we intended or set out to complete, we would have to acknowledge that the lie which told us we were failures was just that -- a lie. And who wants to admit they have been lied to? So we create the conditions of repeated failures in our lives in order to prove we were right all along.

The time to break the cycle is now! The time to dare to be powerful is now! Use your strength in the service of your vision and watch as your life takes off. Because then, it will not matter what failure once felt like, because you will never again be afraid to succeed.

✗ A WARRIOR'S AFFIRMATION ✗

I release from my life the fear of success. I AM successful and know there is nothing to fear because I will never be anything less!

❧ Reflection 32 ❧

"I can accept failure; everyone fails at
something. But I can't accept not trying."

~ Michael Jordan

✗ A WARRIOR'S REFLECTION ✗

One of the greatest signs that we are on the path to success is how often we rise after each and every fall. Why? Because it serves as a testament to where we are in the midst of our journeys.

Rising after a fall is a statement to everyone watching that you are determined to make a mark on this world and refuse to quit in the face of challenges. Michael Jordan is considered to be one of the greatest basketball players to have ever played the game, yet early in his career he failed consistently. However, he never allowed this so called failure to infiltrate his mindset and dictate his life. He developed an incredible work ethic, practiced continually and went on to become the basketball legend he was destined to become.

True failure is not failure simply because you have fallen short of your goals. No, true failure occurs when you accept the lie that you are not nor will you ever be anything more than that particular moment of defeat. It is failure when you allow that voice to dictate your actions for the rest of your life.

What are you destined to become? And, more importantly, what are you willing to do to become it? Success and failure are cut from the same cloth. You are only a failure if you give up and stop trying. And success sits ready at your hand begging you to never give up and to keep going. So, keep going already; because it is in your steady and repeated actions that you decide which part of said cloth you are going to be.

✗ A WARRIOR'S AFFIRMATION ✗

I AM successful at every endeavor that I attempt today. I know that it is more important to keep going and to never give up.

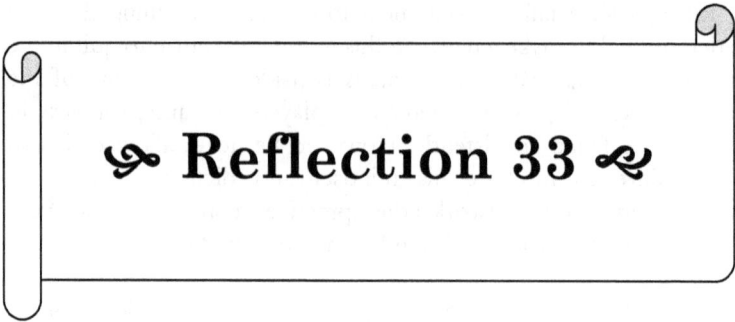

❧ Reflection 33 ❧

"Our chief want is someone who will inspire us
to be what we know we could be."

~ Ralph Waldo Emerson

✗ A WARRIOR'S REFLECTION ✗

Every single person walking this earth is looking for someone to believe in them. Whether we have accomplished a little or a lot, it makes us feel good to know that someone in our lives is looking out for us with every step that we take. And it is the inspiration that we feel in their presence which serves as our muse to continue moving in the right direction.

Yet, many people don't have this? What they have instead are people who tolerate their presence instead of celebrating them. People who do not welcome them with open arms. Who tear down their dreams instead of lending a hand to build them up. Who speak death and defeat over their lives silently hoping they will be forced to live the same pathetic, lonely, dream-deficient life their own lives have become. And actions such as these continues to feed the cycle of doubt and depression. It keeps many in this world off track and forced to live beneath their own standards and inherent potential.

Who are you inspiring today? What dreams do you need fulfilled? Someone out there is waiting for you to inspire them and are looking to inspire you in return. So embrace the words of President Obama and know that "You are the one you have been waiting for". Because once you believe this, you will be able to break the cycle and become a muse thus encouraging someone else to do the same. Now, doesn't that sound inspiring?

✗ A WARRIOR'S AFFIRMATION ✗

Inspiration is my muse. I AM inspired to inspire. I will live the dreams that others don't believe possible so they can believe in themselves and do the same.

❦ Reflection 34 ❧

"I find the great thing in this world is not so much where we stand, as is what direction we are heading."

~ Oliver Wendell Holmes

✗ A WARRIOR'S REFLECTION ✗

No matter how we look at it, life is not about where we are but more so about where we are going. Yet, so many people allow their NOW to create the blueprint for the rest of lives. They allow the moment to speak with such clarity and definitiveness that they stop looking for all the ways they can move forward and they stop seeking the things they need to do to get there.

What causes so many of us to stop moving forward, or to stop believing in a bigger dream, is that we feel lost; we know there is a path and we believe we are supposed to be on said path, but we are long past believing we have what it takes to get there. And this belief finally becomes so strong that we lose focus of the gifts and talents that we possess because we fear we are so screwed up that our gifts and talents do not matter anyway.

You are not lost... you're just looking for footprints. Footprints to either tell you that you are not alone or to remind you that the road was paved long before you got there. It doesn't matter what your life looks like right now as long as you stand strong and acknowledge the journey. Step out in faith and believe that this moment is a part of a much bigger purpose, a much bigger destiny, and you will immediately begin to live a much bigger dream! You are here and it is well!

✗ A WARRIOR'S AFFIRMATION ✗

I AM exactly where I AM supposed to be in my life and the evidence of this lies in my heart. I will continue to take bold steps congratulating myself for not giving up on my journey.

❧ Reflection 35 ❧

"The mind, ever the willing servant, will respond to boldness, for boldness, in effect, is a command to deliver mental resources."

~ Norman Vincent Peale

⚔ A WARRIOR'S REFLECTION ⚔

The language of the mind is that of pictures and it instantly believes that which it sees. It is these pictures and life images that creates the script for how we should behave in situations and circumstances. And it fashions our life's story telling us who we are and how we should believe ourselves to be in the world.

Every time an experience matches a story in our mental rolodex, we automatically behave and act based on the scene that is before us. The only thing that can break this automatic behavior is a gesture or action so bold that it shakes us out of our automated stupor and provides us with the tools necessary to do or to be something new.

To change your story, you have to boldly step off the cliffs of life into the depths of the unknown in order to really see what you are made of. When you do, all of your mental resources will respond to this unanswered challenge and will fill you with a sense of purpose so intense that you will move to a level in life that you have never experienced before.

Aren't you ready to feel the rush of intensity that only a pursuit of purpose can inspire? Don't you want to shake up the monotony in your life and change your story so you can experience something new? Then repaint the pictures you see. Rewrite the stories that shape your life. Step off the cliff and conquer the unknown. And if you fully trust in yourself and your dreams then no parachute is needed! Always remember that your destiny is waiting and be bold! For it is the boldness that is going to deliver the resources you need to conquer this moment in life. You just have to be willing to move. Ready... Set... Go!

⚔ A WARRIOR'S AFFIRMATION ⚔

I AM empowered by the boldness that inhabits my life. I AM
changing my destiny because I AM changing my story.

❧ Reflection 36 ❧

"When life gives you an excuse, give it back.
You don't need it!"

~ Tonoa Bond

✗ A WARRIOR'S REFLECTION ✗

According to Webster, the definition of excuse is "to try to make apology for" or "to try to remove blame from". And in regards to how we live our lives, two of the more impactful definitions are, "to disregard as of trivial import" or "to regard as excusable".

When looking at these four definitions, many of us, without realizing it, live our lives in this vein. We get down on ourselves when the circumstances in our lives do not line up with the vision of what we believe our lives are supposed to be.

And when in the presence of our judges and juries, we approach them with postures of shame and self-contempt seeking desperately for some outside reason as to why our lives did not work out as expected. We stand before them, and the rest of the world, apologetic for being who we are. We inexcusably grant them the inalienable and absolute right to disregard our presence and see us as trivial beings that should be excused from the very liberties life has afforded us all.

Warrior, here is what you have to know and understand today and every day! You are stronger than any excuse life will ever throw your way. When life gives you lemons, don't squeeze the juice into your eyes in order to make yourself cry pitiful and sorry tears; instead make the best tasting, most mouth-watering lemonade you have ever made. Because good things always come out of the so-called B-A-D - as long as you are Bold, Audacious and Determined enough to demand the best out of life that you possibly can.

✗ A WARRIOR'S AFFIRMATION ✗

I AM not the circumstances that have happened in my life. I stand proud of the person that I have become and demand the best that life has to offer.

✺ Reflection 37 ✺

"People are taught that pain is evil and dangerous.
How can they deal with love if they're afraid to feel?
Pain is a feeling. Your feelings are a part of you; your
own reality. If you feel ashamed of them, and hide
them, you're letting society destroy your reality. You
should stand up for your right to feel your pain."

~ Jim Morrison

✗ A WARRIOR'S REFLECTION ✗

Emotions not only rule our behavior but also cause us to both feel and later express that which we are feeling. Yet, so many people attempt to crush the feelings of another; treating their emotions as if they are as dangerous and as life-threatening as the bubonic plague.

We've all seen it before; the father who tells his son that boys don't cry, the boss who fires or disregards the employee as being "weak" for showing emotions while at work, or the friend or family member that teases, whether good-naturedly or not, someone for wearing their hearts/emotions on their sleeve.

And do not dare to tell a pharmaceutically inclined doctor that you experienced an emotion or a pain of any kind, because they will prescribe you something that will rid you of any and all feelings. This way, you can get back to the business of appeasing an expressionless society and being "normal".

Ridding yourself of your ability to feel is in effect like walking around in a zombie like state. It means you're content to live in this world in some unstated and unspoken space, no longer needing to feel alive as long as you are accepted. Being afraid to feel pain means you hold feelings of pleasure hostage too. Stand up for your right to feel something, no matter how painful it is. Stop reliving every day as the night of the living dead. Because it is only in the feeling and expressing of those feelings that you will be able to get on with the business of really and truly living.

✗ A WARRIOR'S AFFIRMATION ✗

My reality is the truth of who I AM. I stand firmly in my resolve that
I feel… therefore I AM!

❧ Reflection 38 ❧

"A man carries in this world that which he carries in his heart."

~ Johann Wolfgang von Goethe

✕ A WARRIOR'S REFLECTION ✕

When you look at the world, what do you see? Do you see a world of empty promises and broken dreams? Or do you see a mountaintop in the hills where an abundance of riches awaits?

Every bitter and painful moment you have endured in your life has built the framework which conditions your every movement. And this has prepared you for your life today. In order for things to change and get better, you have to transform your stories so that you can reflect this change in your heart.

If the mirror of your life is reflecting what you do not want, it is time to change your beliefs so you can change your life! Because in order to have the best, you have to become the best. You have to hold the image of who you are at your best in your mind until you can do nothing else but believe this to be your truth.

You are the sum total of that which you believe. Are you ready to do the work necessary to protect your dreams? Are you willing to do whatever it takes to have all that you have been destined to have? Set your imaginations on high and create within yourself an image that is in line with what you want to become. And when you do, not only will everything that you desire come into your life, but it will remain there as well.

✕ A WARRIOR'S AFFIRMATION ✕

I release all the hurts and pains of the past. I AM the sole protector of my dreams and I AM open to abundance in my life; spirit, soul and body.

❧ Reflection 39 ❧

"Perfect courage means doing unwitnessed what we would be capable of with the world looking on."

~François, Duc de LaRochefoucauld

⚔ A WARRIOR'S REFLECTION ⚔

Perfectionism, or wanting to be perfect, is just a more attractive way of saying fear of failure. One thing that drives our need for perfection is the unconscious desire we have to impress others. But really, the person we should be looking to impress the most is ourselves.

We find ourselves waiting until we have a bigger audience before stepping out and achieving something great. We want there to be a witness to said moment of greatness other than ourselves? And this fear of not being seen causes many to refuse to do anything noteworthy because we do not want to have, be, do or give if no one is there to pat us on the back, sing our praises, and say "job well done."

When a tree falls in the forest and no one is there to bear witness, doesn't it still make a sound? Stop waiting for the perfect moment, the perfect conditions or the perfect time and step out to create these conditions yourself. Do not, for another moment, allow your motivation for life to be tied to the approval of others. Instead, show the world what you are made of. Spend your life in a perpetual state of action. Allow your trees to fall in the forests of your life, and make your dreams come true.

When you look at the spelling of the word "Imperfect", it is clear that this is just another way of saying, "'I'm-perfect' in each and every way." Cheers to you, my friend, for having the courage to be bold in the pursuit of your dreams and to your having an extremely I'm-perfect life!

⚔ A WARRIOR'S AFFIRMATION ⚔

I know that I-AM-perfect just as I AM. I have the courage to pursue my dreams regardless to whether or not anyone is watching.

∾ **Reflection 40** ∾

"People are always blaming their circumstances for what they are. I don't believe in circumstances. The people who get on in the world are the people who get up and look for the circumstances they want, and if they can't find them they make them."

~ George Bernard Shaw

⚔ A WARRIOR'S REFLECTION ⚔

In the beginning was the word and the word was "choice". And what a powerful word it is. What this means is that you can command yourself to become all that you desire to become as long as you step up to the plate of life, make a decision, and do so.

Circumstances in life do not limit your potential; they actually reveal more of who you are. They disclose your true strength of character and show just how resilient you are in the face of troubles. Life is about owning one's choices in order to stand securely in one's power. Blaming your circumstances for where your life is today means you are releasing yourself from your own responsibility to make your life what you want it to be and giving your power to the world.

Each and every decision you have made in your life has brought you to where you are today. Instead of gift-wrapping your power and giving it away by blaming it all on your circumstances, own your decisions and learn the lessons you are meant to learn so you can do in this world what you are meant to do.

The lesson of the week… stop giving your power away! Every single one of us has a little sob in our stories; but not everyone stops and cries over it. The truly successful people make new choices, thus creating the circumstances they need to be successful. So, own your choices, face your circumstances and demand the best that life has to offer. Because you are definitely worth it!

⚔ A WARRIOR'S AFFIRMATION ⚔

I AM confident and assured that I own every action I have taken in my life today. I stand firmly in my power by honoring my choices.

✺ Reflection 41 ✺

"The only people with whom you should try to get even with are those who have helped you."

~ John E. Southard

✕ A WARRIOR'S REFLECTION ✕

If they gave out awards for giving, wouldn't you want the first award to go to you? Whether or not the person you are assisting is someone who has helped you in the past, or if you are paying a prior kindness forward, there is no greater feeling in the world than knowing that what you have done has made someone happier or healthier.

When you avail yourself to helping someone in times of trouble and fulfilling their needs, you receive in exchange the rewards of knowing that you have done your part in healing the ailments present within the human condition. And those witnessing your actions are left with a sense of wanting to live their lives vicariously through you.

Giving really is the best revenge. Helping others is manna to our souls. Yet, anger causes us to miss out on this opportunity when we instead desire to deny goodness to others in an effort to cause them harm. There is no such thing as getting even. When you set out to hurt another, even if this person has hurt you, you place yourself in a negative energetic space rendering you unable to attract the good in your life because it enshrouds you in the bad.

Seek instead to only pay forward the good and you will remain open to the abundant flow of the Universe. Because it is Universal law that as you give so shall you receive… and the Universe always pays forth its debts.

✕ A WARRIOR'S AFFIRMATION ✕

I AM open to goodness in my life. I seek to help others today and give abundantly from my heart.

৯ Reflection 42 ৶

"A journey of a thousand miles begins with a single step."

~ Lao Tzu

✗ A WARRIOR'S REFLECTION ✗

Sometimes it seems as if the road to living our dreams is daunting; especially if the road seems long or seems as if it is going to take longer to get to where we were headed than we want or expect. And this feeling causes us to either rush through the process, or to refuse to move all together, believing that we will never get to where we are going anyway, so why try.

Moving forward in life, and achieving the success we desire, simply requires that we take a series of single steps. That we put one foot in front of the other, while being patient with ourselves, until we make it to our intended destination… no matter how long it takes.

When a child is learning to walk, would you look at that little angel, taking their first triumphant steps, and tell them their progress isn't good enough? Would you tell them their steps are insufficient? Or that since they are walking at a speed that is beneath them they will never, ever, get to where they want to go? I sure hope not, because that would be ridiculous. So then I ask you, why do you do this to yourself?

Stop holding yourself accountable to some unrealistic standard. Your destiny is a foregone conclusion. Therefore, choose to judge your progress for that which it is. Trust that however long the stride or rapid their gait your steps are just the right size for the moment, and you will definitely make it to your intended destination right on schedule.

✗ A WARRIOR'S AFFIRMATION ✗

I AM impressed with my ability to hold my life together. I AM continuing to move forward one step at a time.

❧ Reflection 43 ❧

"The first rule of unleashing your inner warrior
is to know yourself. Because you can't be bold
if you don't know who you are."

~ Tonoa Bond

✗ A WARRIOR'S REFLECTION ✗

Do you remember roll call in grade school where the teacher would call your name and you had to answer to let them know that you were there? The big debate was if one should answer "Here" or "Present". To some, to say the words "I'm here" signifies that you are just barely surviving; that you are allowing for anything life happens to throw your way. But to say, "Present" means you are an active participant in life and are ready to demand all that waits in store for you.

Being present carries with it a sense of awareness. It means you are currently considering who you are and all that you can become. That you have rectified your past with your present and you are taking stock of who you are in the entirety of the situation.

The main questions to ask yourself in any and all situations are, (1) "Who am I?" and (2) "Why do I believe this about myself?" Who are you in said situation, what has happened in your life to convince you to believe this about yourself, and is this belief true? Being present requires that you know who you are every step of the way. And it is in knowing the answers to these questions that you will be able to move forward, conquer your enemies, boldly recreate your life and live your dreams.

✗ A WARRIOR'S AFFIRMATION ✗

I boldly move forward in my life today because I believe the best in and of myself. I know who I AM, why I AM and everything that I stand for.

❧ Reflection 44 ❧

"We are each of us angels with only one wing, and we can only fly by embracing one another."

~ Luciano De Crescenzo

✗ A WARRIOR'S REFLECTION ✗

Life is not so much about independence as it is about interdependence. It is about being there for one another; making the journey of two or more flow seamlessly into one until it is hard to tell where one person's journey ends and the other begins.

Conceptually, to be independent is a great thing. Being independent means, "To be free of another's control" or "Thinking and acting for one's self". And what's wrong with that, right?! Technically nothing. Helping others learn to live up to the standard of these definitions is what I live for. Yet, I also know there is something greater. And this greatness lies in knowing we are "unable to exist or survive without one another."

What life calls forth from us most is a mutual dependence on one another; needing one another for our own sense of survival knowing that the continued existence and evolution of our species and our dreams depends on it. There is someone out there, right now, who needs your wings to help them to fly. And what makes you both equals is that you need them to fly as well.

Don't live your life being independent to a fault. Know that it is okay to look someone else in the eye and say to them, "I need you". And just be patient, because they will eventually reply, "I need you too."

✗ A WARRIOR'S AFFIRMATION ✗

I welcome constructive criticism as feedback for my growth. I AM open to allowing others into my life and know that in sharing our wings we can fly!

ಏ Reflection 45 ೪

"Thousands of geniuses live and die undiscovered - either by themselves or by others."

~ Mark Twain

✗ A WARRIOR'S REFLECTION ✗

Thousands of years ago, the criteria to be a genius was open to all. Today, however, society saves this label for those whom they believe are deserving of it. But true genius defies labels; it knows that in order to be considered great you have to be willing to do something with your life that is so epically inclined that your name and legacy will live on long after you have died a physical death.

So many people are afraid to step outside of the confines of society and boldly live in the realm of genius as they were intended. What they have seemingly forgotten is that our entire reason for living is to fulfill a big, ambitious, larger-than-life, purpose. They allow others to place labels on them while falling captive to the belief that they do not have the necessary tools to live life on an epic scale. They choose instead to believe they are normal; and let's face it, normal people just don't do big things or live big dreams, right?

By the very nature of your being alive, you have genius potential on the inside of you. But unless you do something great - something to express said potential to the ostentatious, flamboyant heights that it should be expressed - this potential will to die with you. Wouldn't you rather instead be remembered for many years to come? Recondition your mindset... shape your destiny... stand in your genius... and live your dreams!

✗ A WARRIOR'S AFFIRMATION ✗

I embody the spirit of greatness that lives within me. I vow that my gifts and talents shall forever express the greatness that I AM onto the world.

❦ Reflection 46 ❧

"It is not because things are difficult that we do not dare. It is because we do not dare that things are difficult."

~ Lucius Annaeus Seneca

✗ A WARRIOR'S REFLECTION ✗

Why is it that for many of us we need some form of the childhood game of "Dare or Double Dare" to tempt us into doing the unimaginable? Without an expressed challenge presented to us, many of us are content to sit back and wallow in the difficulties of life simply wishing things were different instead of rising to the challenge to make them so.

Difficulties arise in our lives mostly out of fear. But just as the common euphemisms goes, "When we fall off a horse we have to get right back on". When life knocks us off our feet, we should not focus only on what was so hard that we failed to succeed. Instead, we must decide that the unconquerable is absolutely conquerable and that we will succeed the more that we try.

Life is unapologetically staring you straight in your face, mocking your fear and applauding your courage. Stand toe to toe with this Giant and dare to do the things that others would never believe are possible. Decide today to boldly stand up to the possibility of failure so that you can succeed beyond your wildest thoughts and imaginations.

No matter how difficult life may seem, it is up to you to do the things that you need to do so that you can have the life that you desire to have. So take a stand and have the courage to be great…I double dare you!

✗ A WARRIOR'S AFFIRMATION ✗

I AM taking a stand to accomplish the things that I once considered daring challenges in my life. I release any fear of the Giant within and welcome its presence in my life on a daily basis.

❧ **Reflection 47** ❧

"Listen, are you breathing just a little and calling it a life?"

~ Mary Oliver

⚔ A WARRIOR'S REFLECTION ⚔

When life smacks us in the face with something we were not expecting, one of the first things that we do is we forget to breathe. We forget that the process of inhaling the good and exhaling the bad is necessary in order for us to live the big, brave, bold lives that we have been destined to live.

Now, this might sound like a strange concept as breathing is an automatic behavior that occurs with or without our approval, but it happens. And it happens more often then many would care to admit. The minute our businesses fail, our children behave in a repugnant manner shaming the family, or someone finds that one skeleton we were sure was well hidden in our closets of despair, we stop breathing and stick our heads in the proverbial sand. We become content to live life as if we are invisible because being seen has proven to be too much to handle.

So I ask you, are you making excuses or are you really living? Are you creating by default or creating by design? Are you bravely becoming or are you simply accepting? And are you living for your dreams or arguing for your limitations? Being bold and audacious is already in your DNA; traits that you simply have to embrace in order to activate. So, inhale the good and exhale the bad and never forget to breathe. Because life is only life when you take a chance and live it!

⚔ A WARRIOR'S AFFIRMATION ⚔

I AM bold in each decision that I make. I inhale the good and exhale the bad knowing that I AM safe and that my dreams are secure.

✎ Reflection 48 ✑

"A coward is incapable of exhibiting love; it is the prerogative of the brave."

~ Mohandas Gandhi

✗ A WARRIOR'S REFLECTION ✗

Love can be a scary thing. Why? Because for many of us we have lived with the belief that certain loves are supposed to be unconditional; yet people within the inner circles of our lives have placed such conditions on them that we no longer know what to believe. So why take the chance of loving someone outside of this circle and getting hurt all over again, right? Wrong!

We are responsible for creating the conditions that we want in our lives, and this is also true where love is concerned. Love is the highest of emotions and when you exude it you show yourself and the world that you are in control of whom you are and who you want to continue to be. Instead of looking at love as something to place a cap on with some while allowing it to be limitless with others, allow yourself to love freely and clearly with everyone at any time.

Don't be a coward. Those who are truly brave couldn't be a coward if they tried. Instead, open your heart and your mind to the possibilities of what loving and being loved by others embodies. It is a beautiful thing to be in control of your emotions, while allowing yourself the freedom of expression to prove it.

✗ A WARRIOR'S AFFIRMATION ✗

I AM open to love… I AM open to being loved… I AM open to giving love… I AM love!

✎ **Reflection 49** ✎

"Never forgetting where you came from is easy.
The challenge lies in never going where you
dreamed of."

~ Phillip Gornail

✗ A WARRIOR'S REFLECTION ✗

When reflecting on the past and what their past means to them, one thing that I impress upon my clients is for them to lose their violins but to keep their stories.

Our stories are the strongest part of who we are; they are wrapped in all that we have gone through as well as all that we have overcome. Our weakest part is the violin that we play, either of our own accord or when society - through some form of self-manipulated pity - tells us that we have the right to play it. And if we're not careful, this melancholy tune will zap our strength leaving us forever singing the battle cry of the weak and weary.

Remembering your story and where you came from strengthens us at our roots. Leaving those roots and never returning, either mentally or physically, is where we are weak and shallow; and these are not traits that we ever want to be. Because when we forget who we are our dreams cease to have meaning and we lose the will and the desire to fly.

Our strength is both in being connected to our past as well as in being connected to our roots. And we become weak and limit our dreams with every strum of the violin. Lose the violins in your life but never, ever give up your stories - for your stories have made you the strong, resilient person that you are today and without them nary a dream in your life is possible.

✗ A WARRIOR'S AFFIRMATION ✗

I AM strengthened by the challenges that I have experienced and overcome in my life. Because of this, I AM empowered to see big visions and to dream big dreams.

✥ Reflection 50 ✥

"Expose yourself to your deepest fear; after that, fear has no power, and the fear of freedom shrinks and vanishes. You are free"

~ Jim Morrison

✗ A WARRIOR'S REFLECTION ✗

Fear, in and of itself, is not real. It is a figment of our imaginations; the thing that we have unknowingly made up and have now given free-reign to run rough-shod over our lives. And this free-reign is based on how we view the world and ourselves in it.

The more control we give to our fears, the more dis-empowered we feel in our lives and this leaves us unable to give our all on the playing fields of life. The remedy for this is to do just as you would if a young child tells you there is a monster under their bed; you would boldly walk into your child's room, flashlight in hand, and shine the light under their bed to give them the proof they need that said monster does not exist. You have to do this for yourself as well; you have to shine the flashlight on your fears and prove to yourself that your fears are self-imposed and that they simply do not exist.

Light is kryptonite to our fears and removes any of the lingering shadows which cause us to give away our power and doubt ourselves. And light in this case is awareness. Once you are aware of your truth and to that which has been revealed, you will see that you are stronger than you give yourself credit for and will realize that there is not now nor has there ever been anything for you to fear. Fear is the only boogey-man... but it is powerful only if you give it power to be.

✗ A WARRIOR'S AFFIRMATION ✗

I stand today empowered to exhibit boldness on the path to my dreams. I know that there is nothing to fear, but fear itself. I AM grateful that I AM free.

❧ Reflection 51 ❧

"A mind, once shaped by a new idea, never goes back to its original dimensions."

~ Oliver Wendell Holmes

✗ A WARRIOR'S REFLECTION ✗

So often in life, we get stuck on a certain idea or philosophy and it takes hardcore evidence to bring us to a moment of awareness in order to persuade us that things could be different.

In order to be aware, you have to be open to the possibilities that exist. You have to be willing to become inspired and know that once inspired always inspired. You have traversed the old, moved into the new and there is no turning back.

Before the 4-minute mile was broken, scientists deemed the body incapable of running a mile in less time. Before the Wright brothers invented the airplane, very few people believed that a contraption so heavy could grace the skies. Before man landed on the moon, space travel was believed to be impossible. Yet, as soon as success in any of these endeavors happened, more people went on to recreate them. Because with valid proof to challenge their beliefs their minds were expanded, and it became impossible to once again hinder them with limitations.

Your mind has already been stretched. The blueprint for change has already been generated. It's time for you to create for yourself what others have deemed impossible. Expand your mind, step into the possibilities, create your destiny and live your dreams.

✗ A WARRIOR'S AFFIRMATION ✗

I AM the creator of my destiny. My mind has been expanded and I refuse to turn back.

❧ Reflection 52 ❧

"Never give up. Let me continue by saying, never, never give up! And in conclusion I say to you, never, never, never, never give up!"

~ Winston Churchill

✗ A WARRIOR'S REFLECTION ✗

The end of Churchill's quote would be a great place to drop in the line, "That is all"; complete with Twitter hash tags (#ThatisAll) and everything that comes with it. After this eloquent command, what more can be said to impart within you the knowledge that you should never give up on yourself and your dreams because the dream is now, and always will be, alive on the inside of you.

You may have had some hard days, and I personally understand how it is the hard ones that can zap the energy right out of you. But just because they're hard doesn't mean you should give up on yourself all together. As long as you are alive and breathing air into your lungs, you should never allow any day that settles into your space to go by unchallenged.

At one point in your life you were fearless. At one point in your life you refused to allow anything to stop you. And if things have changed and if you really are reluctant to live life in a bigger, better and bolder way, then ask yourself what happened and if you really are refusing to. And after you have answered this question then simply redirect, get back on track and continue moving forward.

Mantra of the day: "Never give up! Never, never give up! Never, never, never, never, give up!" #Thatisall!

✗ A WARRIOR'S AFFIRMATION ✗

I AM unstoppable and I AM relentless. I AM determined to succeed and I shall never, ever give up!

109

※ Afterword ※

I recently read a quote from Marsha Norman that says, "Dreams are the illustrations from the book your soul is writing about you." Can't you just hear the power contained within this quote? What this quote is screaming to us all is that everything that we want to be and that we have been created to be is already on the inside of us - and even if we don't always consciously see it, deep inside we really do believe it.

So allow the audacious reflections that you have read to prepare you for your journey; the journey to the inner dimensions of the forever more of your soul. Challenge yourself to allow every dream that you will dream to write your story and create the blueprint of a life that refuses to be denied.

You deserve to live the dreams that legends are made of. You deserve the promises of a destiny that has been written specifically for you. Live your life by the code of audacity and shamelessly and boldly demand the best that life has to offer.

Warrior, the power to become *Audaciously YOU!* is already on the inside of you, and it whispers quiet reminders to you every single time you close your eyes and dream. Now, don't you think that it is well past the time for you audaciously believe it?

✳ About the Author ✳

Tonoa Bond is an author, speaker and Army veteran. She is a prominent mindset coach and mental toughness trainer for elite individuals and teams in the worlds of entertainment, sports, business, multimedia and technology. She is also the CEO and head trainer for McLaughlin-Bond International, a mental toughness coaching and mindset conditioning firm whose roots are based in the combined rudiments of militaristic combat training, behavioral, social & sport psychology, and life skills. Currently, Tonoa is completing a PhD in psychology, focusing on the social and neurological reasoning behind the negative behaviors associated with elite athletes from head-contact prone sports. Founded in research, she believes that with the right mental training, suicide rates, domestic violence, and self-harming behaviors that stem from myriad brain diseases, mood or mental disorders, can be lessened or diminish completely.

Tonoa's life is a testimony to boldness. From the housing projects of Chicago, to the battlefields of the US Army, and later to the halls of corporate America and entrepreneurship, Tonoa cultivated an arrogant disregard towards life's restraints and limitations and has lived her dreams in bigger, better and bolder ways. With over 20 years in the field, she teaches others to do the same. She goes by the moniker of "The Audacity Expert" as she helps individuals to cultivate a shameless boldness and an arrogant disregard for what others may or may not believe is possible and live their dreams bigger, better and bolder than ever before. Her methods empower others to "Unleash the Warrior Within"; to learn key elements of mental toughness and mindset conditioning so they can make the emotional and psychological adjustments in the moment to achieve positive and successful experiences – in life, love and business.

Tonoa conveys her message through part story, part education and sheer magic. So... are you ready to unleash?! Join Tonoa at: www.HouseofWarriors.com.

✳ Acknowledgements ✳

To a few key people, who were strategically placed in my life for such a time as this and for helping volume one of this *Audaciously YOU!* series come to pass.

First, a thank you to the talented word-smith and editor extraordinaire herself, De'Edra Bond-Hodrick - thank you for seeing the things that I didn't see; both in this book and in life. When doing your next puzzle, I have but one word for you... "Whoa".

To my biggest supporter and friend for life, Shibraun Green - how two people as different as you and I became friends is beyond me. Thank you for welcoming me into your family and for showing me early in life that I could fly and for holding that belief until I believed it myself!

Cher Till – Even though you are no longer in this realm with me I still feel your presence. Reflection 44 is dedicated to you! Madame Dragonfly, thank you so much for lending me your wings and helping me to fly! Save a space in Heaven for me!

To my sister-friend for life, Ingrid Sandstrom - WOW! You helped me to remain true to my message of audacity in the face of obstacles. Thank you for seeing and filling a need.

To my family - it took me a long time to really see you, and I am so glad that life circumstances have given me that chance. Thank you all for being you... Audaciously You! Hey, I had to get it from somewhere, right?! ☺

And finally, to all my Warriors out there. Life may be a tough battlefield. Hey, it's supposed to be. But don't ever, ever, ever give up! Because, if you don't fight for your dreams... who will?! You've got this! Shout out if you need me!

❊ Quote Index ❊

In alphabetical order

Peale, Norman V - www.BrainyQuotes.com

Perl, Fritz - www.FritzPerls.com/Quotes

Rand, Ayn - www.BrainyQuote.com

Rockefeller, John D. – www.BrainyQuote.com

Roosevelt, Eleanor - www.ThinkExist.com

Seneca, Lucius Seneca - www.BrainyQuote.com

Shaw, Bernard - www.BrainyQuote.com

Southard, John E. - www.QuotesandPoem.com

Thoreau, Henry D - www.BrainyQuote.com

Twain, Mark - www.TwainQuotes.com

Tzu, Lao - www.ThinkExist.com

Tzu, Sun - www.BrainyQuote.com

von Goethe, Johann - www.BrainyQuote.com